How Do Plants Survive?

Written by Kerrie Shanahan

Series Consultant: Linda Hoyt

WorldWise
Content-based Learning

Contents

Introduction

If you had to name one of the most important things in the world, would you think of plants? If you don't feel that plants are important, just think about this.

We are entirely dependent on plants for food.

Plants, like all living things, grow, **reproduce** and die. They need food to create energy, and they need the right habitat if they are to flourish. However, plants have one amazing difference – they create their own food, and by doing this they provide food and energy for all other living things on Earth.

Plants have one great disadvantage – unlike humans and animals, they cannot move if their habitat changes and no longer provides what they need to survive. When their habitat changes, some plants must adapt. If they cannot, a whole species of plant may die.

But, given time to adapt to their environment, plants can be amazing survivors. They have developed wonderful ways to survive.

How do these plants survive?

These are all plants.

A lithops

A cowberry plant

A sundew plant

A pitcher plant

Chapter 1

What do plants need to survive?

The most amazing thing about plants is that they are able to make their own food. They are the only living things that are able to do this, apart from some **bacteria** and **algae**. All other living things, including humans, depend on plants for their food.

Plants use a gas from the air called carbon dioxide, and water and sunlight. The water and carbon dioxide combine together inside the plant. Using energy from the sun, the water and carbon dioxide turn into a food called glucose. This process is called photosynthesis.

The food that is made is moved around the plant. It moves from the leaves to all parts of the plant through a system of tubes. The plant uses some food to make it grow and stores some of it in the roots, leaves or fruit.

The process of photosynthesis

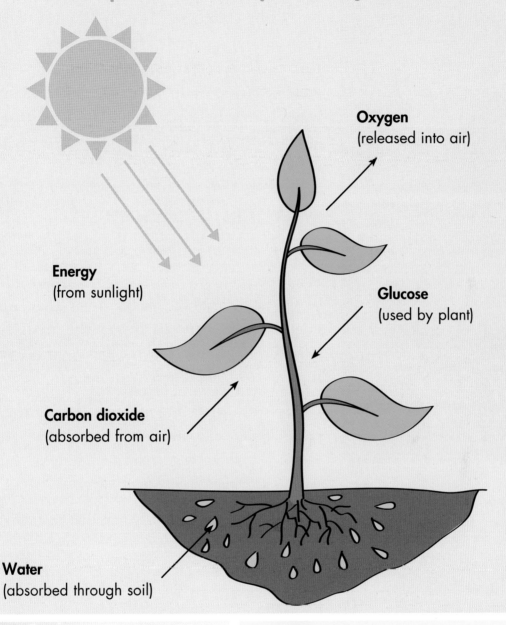

Oxygen
(released into air)

Energy
(from sunlight)

Glucose
(used by plant)

Carbon dioxide
(absorbed from air)

Water
(absorbed through soil)

Did you know?
The word *photosynthesis* can be separated to make two smaller words: "photo" means light and "synthesis" means putting together.

7

How much sunlight do plants need?

Plants need heat and light from sunlight. Different plants need different amounts of sunlight. Some grow well in direct, full sunlight. Other plants grow better in shaded places. Sunlight is important to enable the process of photosynthesis to take place in the leaves of the plants.

How much water do plants need?

Plants need water. In nearly all plants, water is sucked up through the plant's roots. The water is transported to every **cell** in the plant through its tubes. Water is lost from the plant as **water vapour**. It leaves the plant through tiny holes in the leaves.

Water is also needed to keep the plant firm as it grows. Plant cells have a strong, thick wall. When each cell contains water, the plant is upright and strong. If a plant lacks water, it **wilts**.

Plants grow best if they have just the right amount of water. If plants receive too little water, they will **dehydrate** and die. But, if they receive too much water, the roots can become waterlogged, and they can rot, get diseases and die. For example, rice plants grow in water, whereas a cactus can survive on very little water.

Try this

- Fill two glasses of water. Place some red or blue food dye into one of the glasses of water.
- Cut two white flowers off a plant. Place one in each glass.
- Observe what happens in the next few days.
- What does this tell you?

What are nutrients?

Plants usually get their nutrients from soil. Nutrients are components in food that living things need to survive and grow. The nutrients dissolve in water, which is then sucked up by the plant's roots. The nutrients are transported to every part of the plant. Different nutrients help plants with the growth of their roots, seeds, fruits and leaves. Other nutrients help the plant to fight diseases, and some help to keep the plant strong. Some nutrients help the plant with the process of photosynthesis.

Find out more

Soil is a major source of nutrients needed by plants for growth. There are three main nutrients that plants get from healthy soil. Find out what these are. You may like to visit your local garden store to help you investigate.

9

What other conditions are important to healthy plants?

There are certain conditions that allow plants to remain healthy and grow at their best.

Plants need space to grow. If a plant has enough space, it will grow into that space. If a plant is crowded, its growth may be stunted.

Plants need the right temperature. Plants grow best at the temperatures they are used to. If it is suddenly too hot, a plant might lose too much water and wilt. If it is too cold, a plant might freeze.

A healthy plant

A wilted plant

Healthy ecosystem

Did you know?
Plant leaves are made up of very small cells, and inside the cells are a green chemical called chlorophyll, which gives the leaves their green colour. It is the chlorophyll that absorbs the sun's energy.

Plants grow best when they are a part of a healthy **ecosystem**. A healthy ecosystem contains a range of living things that live well together.

Sometimes this balance is upset if a new type of animal or plant is introduced. This can happen when an introduced plant grows so well that it uses up all the needs of the native plants. As a result, some **native** plants die out, and the introduced plant takes over.

Purple loosestrife (*Lythrum salicaria*) is an introduced plant that takes over land.

Chapter 2
Plant adaptations

Plants that grow in places where one or more of the plants' needs are scarce can survive and flourish. They adapt to their environment and develop ways to get what they need.

Lack of nutrients

Many plants live in soils that lack the nutrients they need. They have adapted to these conditions and thrive.

Find out more

Pitcher plants are carnivorous plants. What other plants absorb nutrients by digesting dead insects or other animals?

Pitcher plants

Pitcher plants grow in a range of places, such as sandy meadows, swamps, bogs and marshes. All of these places have poor quality soils with few nutrients. Pitcher plants have adapted to a lack of nutrients in an amazing way – they get the nutrients they need from insects.

Insects are attracted to nectar on the pitcher plant. When an insect lands on the plant, it slides down the smooth inside lip of the flower, and it can't get out. It is trapped. Digestive juices then break down the insect, and the plant absorbs the nutrients.

A fly trapped inside a pitcher plant

Find out more
If tall rainforest trees have a shallow root system, and they grow in wet, soggy soils, why don't they fall over when it is windy?

Tualang trees

Tualang trees grow in rainforests, where they tower over the **canopy**. Rainforest trees grow in poor soils that are very low in nutrients.

The trees have developed a way to get the nutrients they need. They have done this by having very shallow root systems. This means the roots lie just under the ground in the top layer of soil. This layer of soil has the richest supply of nutrients because a large amount of **decaying** plant matter such as leaves, wood and branches constantly falls onto the forest floor. The nutrients remain in the top layer of soil and are absorbed by the roots of the rainforest trees, enabling them to grow strong and tall.

13

Lack of sunlight

Rainforests are full of lush, green plants. Because there are so many plants in a tropical rainforest, there is a lot of competition, especially for sunlight. Many of the plants in a rainforest receive very little sunlight. So, plants growing here have developed other ways to get the sunlight they need.

Giant taros

Giant taros have massive leaves. In fact, they are the largest unsplit leaves of any plant in the world. These large leaves can grow to nearly three metres across. They help the plant get its share of the small amount of sunlight that gets through the thick canopy of the rainforest.

Traveller's palms

Traveller's palms have huge leaves that allow the plant to get as much of the sun as possible. The leaves stand upright with one side facing east and the other side facing west. This allows the leaves to receive sunlight for as much of the day as possible, because the sun's first rays come from the east and the last rays of the day finish in the west.

15

Lack of water

Plants must have water. Some plants grow in places where there is very little water. Most plants would die with such a small amount of water but some survive because they have adapted to having small amounts of water.

Cactuses

Cactuses grow in areas that receive little water. They survive by storing water in their stems. They have few or no leaves, which reduces the area where they can lose moisture. Their roots are usually thin and spread wide to collect any water.

Find out more

The aloe vera is a type of aloe plant. It is helpful to people. Find out how.

Velvet mesquites

Velvet mesquites have adapted to survive with very little water. This shrub grows in a desert where it is dry most of the year. It has developed a deep root system that reaches water a long way underground. These roots can be up to 15 metres deep. They tap into underground water sucking it up so the rest of the plant can use it. It also has a second root system that lies just under the ground to catch any rain that might occasionally fall.

17

Too much water

When a plant is growing in very wet soil, the roots become waterlogged. When roots are waterlogged, oxygen cannot get into the roots, and nutrients cannot be absorbed. Some plants have developed ways to get the oxygen to their roots even when the roots are growing in wet, soggy soils.

Mangroves

Mangroves grow in coastal areas, and their roots are covered in salt water. They have adapted by growing some of their roots above the level of the water. These roots are called aerial roots and they can take in oxygen that travels to those roots that are underwater. This works a bit like a diving snorkel that is partly out of the water, so people can breathe through it.

Mangroves have ways to deal with the salt in the water. They either filter out the salt before the water enters the plant or push the salt into dying leaves that soon drop off.

Pickerelweed plants

Pickerelweed plants grow in water in wetland areas. Like most wetland plants, pickerelweed plants have air sacs or spaces around their roots and stem that trap oxygen. Pickerelweed plants also have hollow stems to transfer oxygen down to the roots.

Summary chart

Problem	Plants		How plants have adapted
Lack of sunlight	Giant taros		Grow on other plants to get closer to the sun Have massive leaves
	Traveller's palms		Leaves face east and west to get maximum sunlight
Lack of nutrients	Pitcher plants		Catch and feed on animals to absorb nutrients
	Tualang trees		Shallow root systems to access nutrients in the top layer of soil
Lack of water	Cactuses		Store water in stems
	Velvet mesquites		Deep underground root system takes in water
Too much water	Mangroves		Roots sit above the water level to take in oxygen
	Pickerelweed plants		Hollow stems to transport oxygen

Chapter 3

From seeds to plants

Like all living things, plants **reproduce**. Many plants reproduce by seeds. The seeds grow on a plant, and when they are ready, they leave the parent plant, **germinate** and begin to grow.

Pollination

Most seed plants have flowers. Flowering plants have male and female parts in their flowers that enable them to reproduce.

Pollen looks like a yellow or orange dust. Pollination happens when the pollen is moved from the male parts of the flower to the female parts. After pollination, a new plant begins to form inside a seed. Most plants then grow fruit around the seed, and this keeps the seed safe.

A young plant growing from a seed

Parts of a flower

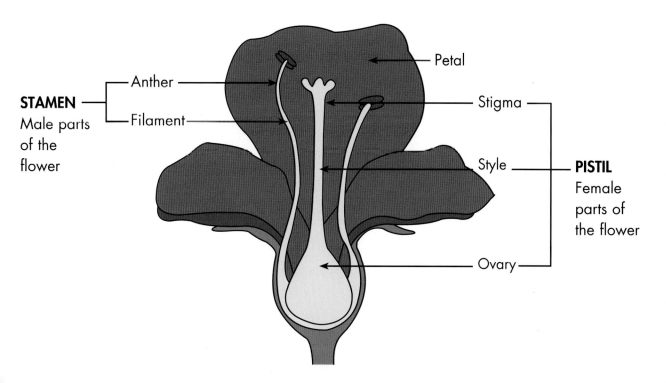

STAMEN
Male parts of the flower

Anther

Filament

Petal

Stigma

Style

Ovary

PISTIL
Female parts of the flower

Attracting animals

Plants rely on animals such as insects and birds to pollinate their flowers. These animals spread pollen from the male parts of one flower to the female parts of another flower.

Plants have ways to attract animals to their flowers so that pollination can occur. Some animals like to eat pollen, which is a nutritious food. They are attracted to the flower's pollen.

Plants that produce nectar, which is a sweet-smelling liquid, attract animals such as bees, birds and butterflies. When the animal drinks the nectar, it might rub against the pollen, and some of the pollen attaches to it. The animal might then rub against the stigma of another flower and leave some of the pollen behind. The pollen then enters the flower, and pollination occurs.

Many flowers have developed bright colours and sweet smells that attract animals and increase the chance of pollination occurring.

Find out more

Self-pollination is when a flower passes pollen from its anther to its stigma. Cross-pollination is when flowers from different plants pollinate. It is better for a plant species to cross-pollinate, so some plants have ways of making sure they cannot self-pollinate. Find out how the avocado and kiwi fruit plants do this.

In Brazil, a skink known as the "little dragon" pollinates the mulungu tree. It laps up nectar from the bottom of the flower of this tree. Pollen sticks to the skink's scales, which is then passed on to other flowers, and pollination occurs. The sugary liquid of the nectar gives the skink the energy and water it needs to survive.

Seed dispersal

Plants have different ways of spreading seeds so that new plants can grow. Some seeds fall to the ground and grow near the parent plant. Other seeds grow a long way from the parent plant. This is called seed dispersal. Seeds can be carried by the wind or in water. Animals also play a role in seed dispersal.

Going for a ride

Seeds that become attached to an animal are carried by the animal to a new place. These seeds called burrs are sticky or have barbs and hooks that stick to fur or feathers. Eventually, the seed falls off or is scratched off. The seed germinates and a new plant grows far from the parent plant.

Dry burdock seeds

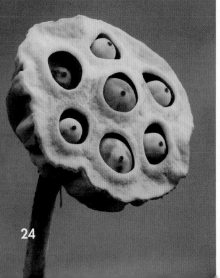

The burrs on this cow contain seeds that stick to its body.

Find out more

The idea for inventing Velcro came from seeds. Find out how.

25

Carried away

Animals such as squirrels and some birds deliberately collect and carry seeds to new places, where they store them to eat at a later time. The animal does not eat all these seeds, and many of these seeds germinate and new plants grow.

Squirrels collect nuts to store over winter. They fail to find all of them later, and the seeds germinate.

Animal waste

Many animals are plant eaters that eat fruits containing seeds. Usually the seeds are too hard for the animal to fully **digest**, and the seed passes through the animal and is released as waste. If conditions are right, the seed will germinate and grow. Often the animal has moved a long way from the parent plant by the time this happens.

Certain seeds germinate more easily after being eaten and expelled by an animal in dung. This is because the process of digestion softens the seed coating, making it ready for germination.

Find out more

How do people play a role in seed dispersal?

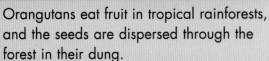

Orangutans eat fruit in tropical rainforests, and the seeds are dispersed through the forest in their dung.

In North Africa, elephants eat fruits, and the seeds are scattered in their dung several kilometres away from the parent plant.

Chapter 4

Amazing plant survivors

Some plants live in places where you would not expect any plant to survive. These plants have developed incredible features that have allowed them to adapt to extreme environments.

Desert holly survives in Death Valley

Plant name: Desert holly

Scientific name: *Atriplex hymenelytra*

Description: A round shrub that grows between 20 and 120 centimetres tall. It has small, pointy leaves and green flowers. It has green or red small, round fruits.

Grows: Grows in desert areas in the United States, such as Death Valley, California.

Conditions: It can grow with very little rain and can **tolerate** salty, sandy soils.

How it survives: It protects itself from the heat of the desert sun. Its leaves grow at an angle, which prevents full sunlight on its leaves at the hottest time of the day. Also, the desert holly is able to extract salt from soil. It uses this salt to cover its leaves and reflect the heat of the sun.

Antarctic pearlwort survives in the coldest place on Earth

Plant name: Antarctic pearlwort

Scientific name: *Colobanthus quitensis*

Description: A tiny plant that grows to just under 5 centimetres tall. It has tiny, green leaves and small, yellow flowers.

Grows: In the Antarctic west coast, where it is slightly milder and has some rain. It is commonly found in rocky areas.

Conditions: It survives freezing cold, windy conditions with little rain, long periods of darkness and poor soils that lack nutrients.

How it survives: It grows close to the ground, often surrounded by rocks, to protect itself from the harsh, freezing winds. It has tiny leaves that minimise water loss. The cup-shaped flowers face towards the sunlight. To pollinate the pearlwort, it must rely on the wind. To maximise the chances of pollination occurring, the Antarctic pearlwort is able to self-pollinate. So, **pollen** need only be blown from one flower to another on the same plant for pollination to happen.

Conclusion

Plants grow all around the world, and they come in many diverse shapes and sizes. But they all have essential things they must have to survive. When the needs of a plant are met, the plant can grow and **reproduce**.

Many plants have developed interesting adaptations to meet their needs. Some of these adaptations are incredible and enable plants to live, even when something that they need for survival is missing in their habitat.

And then there are the survival specialists. These plants live in some of the harshest, toughest places in the world. And they survive! Plants are amazing!

Glossary

algae plant-like living things that can make their own food, mostly found in water

bacteria tiny living things that have only one cell

canopy the highest layer of plants and branches in a forest

cell the smallest unit of a living thing; joins with other cells to make up the living thing, like a "building block"

decaying breaking down slowly into smaller and smaller parts

dehydrate to lose water, and not have enough of it to function properly

digest to break down food into smaller and smaller parts so that it can be absorbed and used by the animal

ecosystem everything in a particular environment, including living things, such as plants and animals, and non-living things, such as water and rocks

germinate when a seed begins to grow into a seedling

native a living thing that originated in the place where it continues to live

pollen tiny, dust-like particles found in plants, that are needed to produce seeds

reproduce when plants make new versions of themselves

tolerate to withstand or live through something without being hurt or damaged

water vapour water in a gas form that spreads out in the air

wilts when a plant becomes limp and droops, due to the loss of water

Index